A Little Kiss Goodnight

Written by
NIELS van HOVE

Illustrated by
C.S. FRITZ

Published in Australia by Truebridges Media

First published in Australia 2021

National Library of Australia Cataloguing-in-Publication entry
Creator: Van Hove, Niels
Title: A little kiss goodnight
KDP paperback: 978-0-6485641-6-4
KDP e-book: 978-0-6485641-7-1
Ingram paperback: 978-0-6485641-8-8
Ingram hardback: 978-0-6485641-9-5
Target Audience: Newborn, infants, toddlers
Subjects: Children's bedtime story, stories in verse

Cover layout and illustrations by C.S. Fritz
Typesetting by Nelly Murariu (PixBeeDesign.com)
Printed by Kindle Direct Publishing & Ingramspark

This book belongs to:

Who loves

a little kiss goodnight!

All around the
world when
the moon
is shining bright.

Parents give their children

a little kiss

goodnight.

Some children will be crying,

some are *snuggled*

up tight.

They all are looking forward,

to a *little* kiss

goodnight.

Some children sleep in

busy cities...

Some in hills high

or valleys down low ...

Some sleep near
sunny sand...

Some sleep near *icy* snow.

And all of those children,
to everyone's delight.
Will get from their
parents, a *little*
kiss goodnight.

Some children feel tired,
eyes *heavy* as stones.

Some will be restless,
with an *itch* in their bones.

Some children *resist*.

they don't want to let go.

Some *laugh* and *giggle*,

and go with the flow.

What they all have *in common*,

if it's wrong or if it's right.

They love their parents,
to give a *little kiss goodnight.*

But you are
my treasure,
you're mine in
every way.

I will *kiss you goodnight* as long as I may.

'Cause time keeps on flying and
you'll be grown soon.
Until the day comes,
that you look up to

the moon.

When you *hold* your *baby*, and stars are shining bright.

You'll remember I was always there...

... to give a

little kiss goodnight.

About the author

Niels lives in Melbourne, Australia. He is an author who tries to make a positive difference with his books and help children learn about confidence, resilience and a positive mindset. He is also a father of two girls who he has kissed goodnight almost every single night of their lives.

Other books by Niels

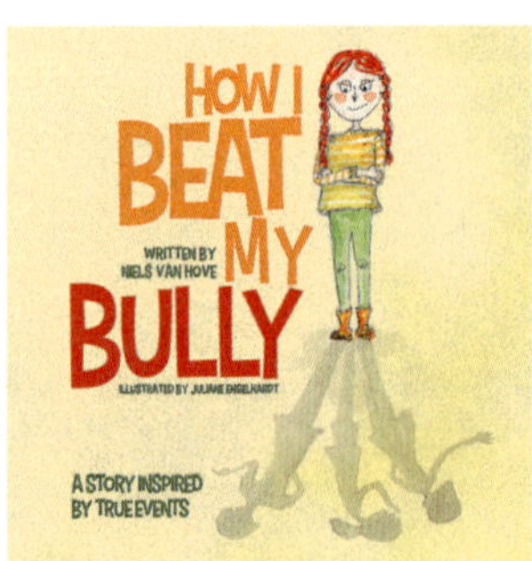

About the Illustrator

C. S. (Casey) Fritz writes and illustrates full time and is the creator of *Seekers*, *Good Night Tales*, the *Cottonmouth* series, *Good Night Classics* and much more. Casey and his wife, Emily, have been married since 2005 and have a son and a daughter.

Made in the USA
Monee, IL
22 October 2021

80582555R00021